NYLAH Vs GERMS
A.J Gholson
HYGIENE 17
HYGIENE
HYGIENES 19
HYGIENE 6
YGIENE 1
Follow Nylah
@nylahversus

Covid has really taught Nylah the importance of hygiene

and that in order to stop the spread we must all work as a team.

So whenever Nylah goes out
one of her biggest concerns is
that she and her family stay safe
from germs

Germs can cause sickness like the flu or a cold

So Nylah practices safety through a ryhme she was told

We wear a mask
and keep our space
then wash our hands
before we touch our face

And now that the team knows the best way to score,
she and her dad are headed to the store

A full parking lot shows the crowd is live

So Nylah puts on her game face the moment she arrives

A coin is needed before the game can start

So her dad uses a quarter
to take a cart

Now with the ball in Nylah's possession, germs rush at her from every direction

10
Though you can't see germs and
they never make a sound,
no matter where you are
they're always around

But whether on the floor, wall,
or even in the air, the safety Nylah
has won't let germs near.

Being careful to avoid dirty surfaces
and such, Nylah makes her way down
the field and she can't be touched

20
And when there are people in the aisle
blocking the path

Nylah waits for an opening
before she goes to pass

Once it's time to check out
Nylah knows the role

A six foot distance brings her
closer to the goal.

Since mask pulling is against the rules

She keeps it on until they're ready to cruise.

Touchdown!!!
HYGIENES
HEALTHY!
MUCUS 4
BACTERIA 25
DROPLETS 15
SANITIZER 20

Nylah makes it home just as planned

And earns extra points
by washing her hands.

say hello to
Professor Nylah.

www.ingramcontent.com/pod-product-compliance
Lightning Source LLC
Chambersburg PA
CBHW042159030726
47599CB00004B/795